ETHEREUM INVESTING

A COMPLETE BLUEPRINT TO UNDERSTANDING AND PROFITING WITH ETHEREUM:

GETTING RICH FROM BLOCKCHAIN CRYPTOCURRENCIES

BY RICHARD HAYEN

Disclaimer

TABLE OF CONTENTS

INTRODUCTION

Congratulations on downloading your personal copy of Ethereum Investing. Thank you for doing so.

The following chapters will discuss some of the many ways that you can invest in Ethereum. You will discover how important it is to make sure that you are investing in all of the right things. The final chapter will explore the future of Ethereum and what it will mean for investors just like you.

By the end of this book, you will be able to effectively capture the investment opportunity that lies in Ethereum. You can make sure that you are getting the best deal possible on the investment, learn how you can use it while it is in your possession, and discover how you can sell it for profit.

There are plenty of books on this subject on the market, thanks again for choosing this one! Every effort was made to ensure it is full of as much useful information as possible. Please enjoy!

CHAPTER 1: WHAT IS ETHEREUM?

There is no way that you can expect to start making money on Ethereum if you don't even know what it is. It is a simple concept that has somewhat complicated origins, and you need to make sure that you know as much about it as possible before you invest in it. Like all types of investing, you should have a good idea of what the product is and what you can do with it to make sure that you are getting the most out of the experience.

Ethereum is very similar to Bitcoin in that it is a cryptocurrency. It is something that is not necessary "real" in a third-dimension sense, but it is certainly real in that it is making actual money for people who have chosen to use it and for people who have chosen to invest in it. Ethereum is a simple way of making money, trading money and profiting off of the money.

One of the best parts about Ethereum is that it can be used for many different purposes. It is most commonly used on Internet platforms and very tech-savvy stores, but it can also be used for other purposes. There are many ways that people choose to use it. The most common happening with Ethereum is purchasing it at a low cost, allowing it to sit in an account for a short period and then selling it off for a higher profit.

With Ethereum, you never actually have to touch the money. Since it is a currency, it is something that is all handled online and something that can be traded online without ever having to worry about the different problems that can come with different amounts of other types of money. You don't have to even see "real" currency until you are ready to cash in on the currency that you have built up with Ethereum. One of the best things about it is that you can even hold onto it and buy everything from simple tech gadgets to boats and even homes.

Another thing that is great about Ethereum is that it is not regulated by the government. While there is a chance that this will not last forever, it is something that people can enjoy for the time being. They do not have to worry about reporting the Ethereum that they get and it was not created by the government. Similar to Bitcoin, the government does own some Ethereum, but that simply means that they are collectors of this excellent investment just like everyone else who is in on the action.

Ethereum is easy to manage and to handle. It can be converted very simply into other types of currency and all you need to do is make sure that you are getting the best opportunity possible out of the options that you have. For example, once you have purchased the Ethereum, it is all going to be in the same place. This is your virtual wallet and it is associated only with your ID number. It does not have your name on it and the chances of anyone figuring out your real identity from the ID number are very slim.

The prices of Ethereum are quickly rising as it becomes more popular and because of the different things that are going on with it. This is something that is a direct result of the free market on it as an investment portion. This is something that you need to keep track of and something that you should know about before you try to do different things. When it comes to Ethereum, like most forms of investing, you should purchase it for as low of a price as possible and then sell it off for as high of a price as possible so that you can truly invest in it.

Since there are so many different aspects to Ethereum and to investing in it (as well as profiting from it), you will be able to learn as much as possible from this book. The information that is included here is meant to help you make a lot of money. While we can't guarantee that you will become rich from Ethereum, we can give you the information that you need and the tools required. The work that you do to get rich is up to you!

CHAPTER 2: THE SECURITY OF ETHEREUM

As with most things that are included with the Internet, many people wonder how secure Ethereum is. As a currency that is unregulated and with things that are essentially crowdsourced, it can be easy to think that Ethereum is not exactly the most secure option for you to invest in. While it is true that many people are concerned about the security of it and the ability to invest in it without a huge amount of risk, there are certain things that can make people feel better about what they have to do with Ethereum and how it can make them build up a huge amount of profit from it.

THE APPLICATION

There is an application that everyone who uses Ethereum will need to use. This is how they buy the currency, how they allow it to sit and how they can sell it off. It is important that people make sure that they can get the Ethereum that they need without having to worry about the problems that come along with having several different applications that are required to use it.

YOUR IDENTITY

One of the best parts about it is that your identity will always be protected. While you may need to invest in it by associating your application with a bank account, there is a process that scrambles that information between when you put the money in (or take it out) and when you are investing in the Ethereum. It is important to note that you are still traceable for the purchases that you make but that your security will always remain a high priority when it comes to Ethereum.

HAVING A WALLET

The wallet that you have with all of your Ethereum in it is included with the application. It is something that is easy to use and something that you will be able to get a lot of benefits from. This is something that is beneficial for nearly everyone who uses the app and something that makes it easier for you to make the right investment choices. There are many options for keeping your money secure in your wallet but simply having one that is available in your application is one of the best ways to stay secure.

ENCODED MONEY

All of the "money" that you have in Ethereum is encoded. Each piece of Ethereum has a special code that is associated with it. It is easy to make sure that you know which money is yours and if something happens to it. A great benefit comes from being able to make sure that you are going to get the true best options from the Ethereum codes. For example, if someone were to steal your Ethereum (highly unlikely), you would be able to trace it back to the person using the coding that the money has that is associated with it in the Ethereum world.

PREVENTING THEFT

Preventing theft is easy with Ethereum. Simply do not share your password to the application with anyone. This is where all of your money is stored and where it will be kept the same because of the things that are associated with it. It is important to know that you will need to make sure that you are going to get the most out of Ethereum and that you are going to be able to actually invest it each time that you want to do different things. Make sure that your password is strong and that you don't let anyone know what it is.

HACKING PROBLEMS

In the past, there were problems that came with the hacking of the application. This resulted in people losing a portion of their investment but it is something that they also fixed quickly. The developers of the application are constantly working to make sure that it does not happen anymore and that you are protected while you are using the application. There should be nothing to worry about when it comes to hacking because you will always be protected with the app and with the people who work to make sure that the app is secure for you to use while you are investing in Ethereum.

SPENDING IT

Spending Ethereum is relatively simple and can be done without much hassle at all. You only need to use your wallet to be able to spend it and then you actually only need your ID. You would simply enter it into the algorithm and then you could spend the Ethereum. This is not necessarily something that you would want to do with it all of the time because the value is always changing. It is much better to simply buy Ethereum, hold onto it until the price rises and then sell it for a profit. Then, use that profit to buy whatever it is that you were going to buy with Ethereum.

COMPARE TO CREDIT CARDS

Most people who use their credit cards online think that they are safe because the site is secure or because having that card gives them a false sense of security. The truth, though, is that you are not secure using your credit card for some of the purchases that you make online. The increase in credit card theft and identity theft is likely because many people use their card on sites that are less than reputable. With Ethereum, you don't have to worry about your identity getting stolen.

SOLID INVESTMENT

Security is also important when it comes to investing. Ethereum is a good investment because it has been steadily rising in value in the time that it has been around. It has not had a major drop at nearly any point and the majority of people who have invested in it are now profiting from it. Because of this, you can make sure that you are getting the best and most secure investment possible. The chances of someone stealing your investment in Ethereum are low but the chances of losing money from it are also very low.

CHAPTER 3: ETHEREUM VS. BITCOIN

It is hard to talk about currency and to invest in cryptocurrency without bringing up some of the facts that come along with it. For example, Bitcoin is one of the most popular options for people who want to invest in this type of currency. Bitcoin is popular because of the availability of it, and it is something that many people can benefit from. There are some problems with Bitcoin, though. Ethereum is something that can solve the majority of these problems for people who invest in Cryptocurrency.

BITCOIN

APPLICATION

The application that is used for Bitcoin is run by a single person. It is one that is monetized and it can be complicated to use. The people who run it have a hard control on the market and they are able to make the money that comes from it through the different processes that they have. It is easy for people to use and it is something that most people need to make sure that they are taking advantage of.

PURCHASE

There is a different process for purchasing Bitcoin. It is complicated and involves a waiting period, often. Sometimes, if you decide to not use the waiting period, you will not be able to get the Bitcoin that you want. You will also need to make sure that you are using a bank account instead of a debit card so that you can purchase as much as possible. People who try to do it with a credit card will struggle to be able to get the Bitcoin that they want and they may not be able to have the best experience possible with their Bitcoin.

STABILITY

There is a lot of stability in the e-currency market but Bitcoin has seen a lot of change in the years that it has been present. For example, the percent that it grows on a yearly basis can vary depending on the time and the situation that the economy is in. There has been steady growth but that growth has not been uniform and it is hard to predict what type of growth there is going to be in the future for Bitcoin and with the different things that are associated with it. It is not something that is going to come down too much in value but you will never know how much it is going to increase depending on the time.

RESALE

Similar to everything else that happens with Bitcoin, it can be complicated to resell the Bitcoin. You may struggle to make your money back from selling, and this can be a huge problem for people who want to turn around and make a lot of money. The idea of day trading Bitcoin can be complicated and is not always the best thing for people who want to make money. For this reason, day traders should stay away from Bitcoin and from what it has to offer people.

MARKET

The market for both is relatively similar. The biggest problem with Bitcoin is that it is offered in multiple retail formats. For example, you can buy Bitcoin from, at least, three different websites. You will then have three different wallets that your Bitcoin is in, and you will have to manage the Bitcoin from each of these locations. The market is huge with this, and it can get complicated especially if you have several different wallets. You will also have to remember the terms and costs for each of the places where you have purchased your Bitcoin.

ETHEREUM

APPLICATION

The application that people use to manage their Ethereum is simple and is open source. This means that it does not have just one owner but that most of the investors who use it are owners of the app. This is something that is nice, and it allows Ethereum to be able to be offered in many different (and exciting) ways for the users of the app. There is only one app that people can manage Ethereum from which reduces the confusion that sometimes comes with cryptocurrency. You must use the same app that everyone else is using.

PURCHASE

To purchase Ethereum, all you have to do is get on the app and purchase it. You can use a debit card that is associated with a bank account or simply a bank account. The app suggests that you use a bank account to make it easier to transfer and to eliminate some of the fees that come along with debit card usage. It is up to you, though, what you do with it and how you manage it. When you are using Ethereum, you should use the bank account and try to eliminate at least one of the middlemen in the process.

STABILITY

Ethereum has had about the same amount of growth in the time that it has been on the market. This means that it has steadily risen almost every day in the past that it has been able to be used. It also means that it has been able to make a difference with the options that it has for people. With the stability that is offered in Ethereum, you can make sure that you are getting the best experience possible. You can also make sure that you are going to know what the growth is going to be in the coming years.

RESALE

As with everything else that is done with Ethereum, you can sell it on the app. You can sell it back to the app for a trading fee or you can choose to sell it to someone else who wants to buy into Ethereum. There is almost always a fee associated with reselling it (just like with real money investing) so you should make sure that you are preparing for that when you are considering the profits that you get with the options that are included.

MARKET

The market for Ethereum is much simpler than the market for Bitcoin. There is only one place that you can buy it from, and this is the only thing that you will need to do. The application is the only place that you can get Ethereum, and you need to make sure that you are doing everything else that is included with the application. It is a good idea to make sure that you are keeping the application at all times because you will do everything from managing the money on it to selling it and even purchasing more. The simplicity of using the app allows you the chance to spend more time building up your Ethereum stock and less time searching for the best price.

CHAPTER 4:

UNDERSTANDING VIRTUAL MACHINES

The majority of things that will go on with your Ethereum involve the use of a virtual machine. This is something that you need to make sure that you are able to do and something that is able to provide people with the options that are included in computing software. It is also something that is somewhat complicated to understand because there is no physical computer that is associated with it. By looking at the different things that are associated with virtual machines, you can understand the way that they are used to manage Ethereum.

PHYSICAL COMPUTER

The physical computer that you use is made up of working parts and is able to be used based on the different things that you may be able to do it. This means that you need to make sure that you are doing things the right way and that you will be able to include all of the different options that come with computers. There are many different options for people who want to be able to use their computer and who want a physical computer. It is important to make sure that you know how a computer works and that it involves both hardware and software to make sure that it is working in the right way.

SOFTWARE

The software that is on your computer is designed to make it easier for you to do different things. From the way that you can do things like creating word processing documents to being able to use the Internet, this can all be attributed to the software that is included with your computer. You need to make sure that you have the right software and that it is all being used in the right way. If you do not have that software, your computer will not be able to work in the way that you want it to. The same goes for virtual machines and the way that they are able to be used for different abilities.

HOSTING

Despite the fact that a virtual machine does not have a physical location that it is in, it still has a host that it is in a physical location. This is where the storage for the computer is located at and where it is able to be used for different things. It is important to note that there are many different options when it comes to physical computers but the majority of them are added to be able to provide people with the options that are included. For example, you will need to make sure that you know where your virtual computer's physical host location is so that you can make sure that you are getting all of the help that you want from the specific computer along with everything that the machine is able to provide to you.

IN A LOCATION

The location that the host is in should generally be the same country that the virtual machine is working from. This means that the virtual machine should not have a host that is thousands of miles away and it should not be something that is hard for people to understand each time that they do different things with their hosting software. It is also something that will enable people to be able to get the right type of options for their computer hosting along with the virtual machine assistance. Make sure that you are aware of everything that goes into your computer long before you make the decision to use the computer.

ADDITIONAL OPTIONS

One of the best options that you can choose from is to make sure that you are using the app from the host that it is on. This is something that will allow you the chance to make sure that you are getting what you can from the application and that Ethereum is going to make the most sense possible. There is a lot that goes into the app and this means that you need to make sure that you will be able to do the most with it. It is something that can be thought of as an application process and something that needs to be dealt with according to the different options that are included with the Ethereum application.

CHOSEN SERVERS

The servers that the virtual machine is on are different than ones that a physical computer is able to use. This is because the people who created the virtual machine wanted to make sure that it was up to their demands and that the application would be able to be used the correct way. There are many options for people who want to use the Ethereum application but all of these people will need to make sure that they are going to be able to do the best job possible with what they have to work with.

APPLICATION HOSTING

Hosting an application is somewhat different than hosting a website or something that is similar to it. This is because the application hosting process requires that people work to make sure that they are going to be able to do everything that they can with the application that they have. It is something that will change the way that things are done and something that will make it easier for the people who want to be able to host the application. There are many different parts to the application and they are all hosted on different servers.

CHAPTER 5:

WHAT ARE USES OF ETHEREUM?

Ethereum, like most other cryptocurrency options and things that are similar, has many different uses. These are all things that people can use the currency for, and this allows it to be easier for them to make sure that they are going to be able to do what they can to add different things to the experience. There are many things that people can do to make sure that they are going to be able to have the best experience possible with Ethereum. When you are considering Ethereum and purchasing some of the cryptocurrency, you should always consider the various uses of it.

INVESTMENT

The investment process is something that everyone will need to go through. It is also something that happens automatically when you buy Ethereum. From the time that you buy it until you spend it, it increases in value and is something that will allow you the chance to truly be able to get the most out of the process. There are many different options that are included with Ethereum and that allows the people to be able to get things started when it comes to their investments.

When you make the decision to invest in Ethereum, you will be able to purchase it and then resell it at a higher price. This is what the majority of people do when they purchase

Ethereum. It is also something that allows you the chance to make money. Some people make money almost exclusively with these options, and it allows them the chance to truly enjoy Ethereum.

If you are going to use Ethereum, this is one of the most profitable ways to do it and will help you to make the most amount of money possible.

SPENDING

Some people choose to use Ethereum in the same way that they use Bitcoin. They use it to be able to spend it, and that is something that they will make sure that they can do in all situations. There are many different options that are included with the spending, but some people may benefit more from not spending the money than if they were to spend it. This allows them the chance to make sure that they are going to be able to get the most out of the money. Since it is so high priced, Ethereum can sometimes be hard to be able to spend money.

When you are working to make sure that you are using Ethereum in the right way, you need to do everything that you can to be able to add the different options to your spending habits. Since Ethereum can be construed as somewhat of an expensive option, you may want to consider using it for something that is not related to spending.

It is also difficult to find someone who accepts Ethereum as currency. While Bitcoin is even more popular than Ethereum, it is still only accepted at a few places where people can use it to buy things like tech-related items and others.

COLLECTIONS

One thing that some people may want it for is collecting it. This is associated with another option, like investing it and trying to get more money out of it. Not everyone can get the most out of it, and some people choose to have it for that purpose only – just to have it.

When someone wants to use it for a collection, they will not be able to use it for different purposes. This is often the case with people who are very tech-savvy and people who simply enjoy having nice things. It is something that others can do, but many choose not to because it isn't the most profitable way for you to use the money that you made from Ethereum. The collecting aspect of it is great but it is not profitable, and it is not something that most people would choose to be able to do.

There are many different options when it comes to investing in Ethereum but collecting it is one of the most closely associated options. You can make sure that you are doing things the right way and that you are adding different options to your Ethereum collection. It will enable you to figure out how you can then get rid of your collection for money.

TECHNOLOGY

Those who are interested in Ethereum are closely associated with technology. This means that the majority of people who collect it are those who want to be able to get more out of it. When you are collecting Ethereum, you are collecting a piece of technology. It is something that you can use and something that you can become more comfortable with when you try to make the right decision for your experience. There are many different options that come along with Ethereum, but nearly all of them are things that you can get the most out of.

If you are interested in technology and you like to learn a lot about it, consider Ethereum. You can try to make sure that you are getting the most out of it each time that you do something new. You will be able to truly benefit from Ethereum, and that will give you a chance to do more with what you have. It is always a good idea to try new things because that is how new technology is created.

All of these reasons are great for people who want to use Ethereum. They all make sense in their way, and they are all able to include the various options for investing. It is a great way for people to be sure that they are getting what they can from the process. It is also something that will allow them the chance to make sure that they are doing everything that they can with the various prices associated with Ethereum.

Chapter 6: The Pros and Cons of Using Ethereum

As with most things, especially those that are technology-related, there are pros and cons to using Ethereum. These are made up of different things that you will need to make sure that you are doing right and that you can be sure you will be able to change bout the different things that are included with your experience in cryptocurrency. We'll take a look at the definitive pros and cons to using Ethereum as opposed to using another form of cryptocurrency or nothing at all.

Pros

CONTRACTING

The contract that Ethereum is under is one that is meant to protect the consumers and the people who use it in the way that it was intended for. Unlike Bitcoin, Ethereum has capabilities that are linked to being able to do different things. It is something that had enabled people to make the right choice with the money that they have and with the investing opportunities that they had created when they were doing different things. Because of the various options that are included with Ethereum, people can get the best response possible with their investment technology.

APPLICATION

Since the application is not decentralized, it is something that will change depending on the different aspects of the way that it is being used. This simply means that there is not a single entity that controls it. While some may think of this as somewhat of a negative aspect to using the app and having it available to them, it is something that will work better for the people who are doing various things. When you are using the decentralized version of the app, you will not have to worry about whether the owner has ulterior motives or not.

DESIGN OF APP

The thorium is the way that you can mine for the Ethereum. It gives you the chance to make sure that you are designing things the correct way and that you will be able to add all of the various services to your experiences. You should make sure that you are going to be able to do a lot with the app and that you are going to be able to find the exact mine that you want to be able to get the Ethereum. This is, of course, if you plan to mine for it. If you are not planning on mining for Ethereum and simply want to purchase it for resale so that you can profit off of it, this would not apply. It is worth mentioning, though, that mining is the best way to make the highest profit possible with the Ethereum.

CONS

NEWNESS

Bitcoin is a new concept. It is so new that many people do not even have it listed on their site and some have never even heard of it. This is mainly a problem for the people who want to be able to get the best experience possible out of cryptocurrency. It is something that needs to be done the right way and something that will change depending on what you want to do. If you are going to use Ethereum, it is worth noting that it is even newer than Bitcoin. Some people have never even heard of Ethereum and even fewer people have the capability to accept it for payments. Be aware of each of these things when you make the decision to invest in it or when you want to use it for purchases.

CENTRALIZATION

The centralized idea of Bitcoin is that it can be hard to make sure that you are getting the best experience possible. For example, you need to make sure that you are going to be able to include everything that you need with the Bitcoin that you have. You also need to make sure that the centralized idea of Bitcoin does not include major problems for you if you are going to be investing in it. While the application is decentralized, many of the things that go into the application are not. The money still has centralized tendencies, and it has to be taken care of each time that you make the decision to do different things with it.

INFLATION

Looking at Ethereum, especially for spending as opposed to investing, requires that you recognize the different things that go into it. The inflation of Ethereum is much higher than Bitcoin although it is not quite as high as it is with traditional forms of money. You should make sure that you are prepared for the higher inflation when you make the decision to invest in Ethereum so that you are not shocked by the outlandish things that happen when you try to purchase something with it.

UNDERSTANDING

It is very difficult to understand the way that Ethereum works. If you do not have a background in the technology field, you may struggle to figure out the way that Ethereum works. If you think that it seems complicated, that is because it is. You need to make sure that you know about Ethereum before you invest in it. While Ethereum is complicated, Bitcoin is equally as complicated. All cryptocurrency is but if you take the time to learn more about it, it will be much simpler for you to figure out the right way to do it.

INVESTMENT

There are many different ways that you can make an investment in Ethereum. This is because of the various options that are included in the investment process. It provides you with the opportunity to do more and to learn more about what you are doing as well as the various aspects that go into using the product. If you want to make sure that you are investing things in the right way, you should make sure that you are going to be able to include everything with the investment. It is a good idea to try and figure out an investment strategy before you start to invest in it.

CHAPTER 7:

THE PROCESS OF BUYING ETHEREUM

There are certain steps that you will need to take if you are going to buy Ethereum. Whether you are buying it to use in the virtual world or you are buying it to try and invest in it, you will need to take these steps to figure out the right way to do all of it. This is the easiest way to ensure that you are going to be able to get the most out of it.

ACCOUNT

The first thing that you will need to do is have a bank account. You can either use an actual bank account to be able to pay for the Ethereum, or you can use a debit card associated with your bank account. It is not a good idea to try to use a credit card to invest because of the problems that are associated with charging investments to a credit account and having to turn around and pay your bills with the credit card along with paying the actual credit card bills.

DOWNLOAD THE APP

Anyone who has Ethereum has to use the application that is associated with it. This is because it is made to be used with it and it is something that you will need to make sure that you are doing in the right way. If you do not have the application, you simply cannot purchase it. This is something that you can either put on your smartphone or your tablet. You can also use a desktop application, but this is not as intuitive as the other application options.

Make an Account

Once you have downloaded the application for Ethereum and you have it on your phone or your tablet, you will need to make an account on the site. This is something that will give you the chance to do more with the application and will also allow you to set up your information. You can pick and choose which information you want to include at the beginning, but you should know that, in order for your wallet to truly work, you will need to provide the rest of the information on the application so that it can use your information for various things on the application.

Connect with the Bank

Be sure that you always have your account connected with your bank. Whether that is in the form of your actual account or your debit card is inconsequential. This is where the real difference in Ethereum and Bitcoin lies. With Bitcoin, you can only add a certain amount of money with a debit card before you have to pay for the extra services with your bank account. It is a good idea to try and make sure that you are doing everything that you can with your chosen specifics. There are many options for Ethereum purchasing, but they all involve having a bank account.

PROVIDE CREDENTIALS

Your credentials are needed to get your account setup. If you put all of your information into the account when you first started your Ethereum application account, you will not have to worry about the problems that come with this step. If you did not, it is now time to start entering your information into the application so that you will be able to get the biggest benefit out of using the app. Be sure that you put everything into the app accurately so that you don't have to worry about the app not recognizing who you are.

CHOOSE YOUR WALLET

You can pick and choose the different options for your wallet. You need to make sure that you are prepared with the wallet of your choice and that you are doing what you can to make your wallet work. There are different settings that are associated with wallets on the Ethereum app so make sure you choose the one that will work the best for you. You should always work to make sure that things are going to be included with the application and that you will be able to do everything that you can with your application. It is imperative that you use the app in the right way.

PURCHASE THE MONEY

This may seem like a strange thing, but you will need to purchase the Ethereum. Despite the fact that it is a currency, it is still encrypted, and you need to make the purchase to be able to get it. You will then be assigned the chosen number of Ethereum coins that you want. Each one of them will have different amounts that are associated with them, and you will be able to use them in the way that you want – whether that is for investing or for spending at online retailers.

CREATE OPPORTUNITIES

The opportunities that you have for spending your Ethereum are all different depending what you have and what you want to be able to do with it. This is something that will change depending on the different options that you have, and it will make a lot of difference in your lifestyle. The Ethereum that you have used in the past will all be tracked and added to different things so that you can learn what you need to know about your investment and the various sales that you have. Be sure that you work to figure that out.

ADDITIONAL INFORMATION

The information that you have on the Ethereum that you have in your possession will change depending on the different things that you want to be able to have. It is a good idea to make sure that you know what you are doing when you are making the changes to your Ethereum account. It is also a good idea to try different things so that you will be able to get more out of the experience. When you are using Ethereum, know that information will be the best way to figure out how to use it and what you can use it for. Keep your eye out for new places that are constantly accepting the latest form of cryptocurrency.

Chapter 8: Tips and Tricks for Ethereum

When you are first getting started with Ethereum, there are quite a few things that you will need to know to make sure that you are going to be able to get the best experience possible. It is important that you follow each of the directions with Ethereum so that you will be able to get a better experience. It is also necessary for you to make sure that you are getting what you can out of Ethereum. By following these tips and tricks, you can find the right way to invest in (and spend) Ethereum.

Invest in It

The investment aspect of Ethereum is the biggest and best thing that you will be able to do with the e-currency. It is important because you can make a lot of money from it but it is also important because it is something that most people do with it. You can make a lot of money from it if you just work to make sure that you are getting the best and biggest profit available.

Make the Time for It

Investing takes a lot of time. Be sure that you are prepared for that. Even with investing in Ethereum, you will still need to dedicate a certain amount of time if you want to be able to get the best experience possible. While it is not wise to dedicate entire days to investing at this point in your investment career, you should still work to try and make some time for it. Set aside an hour or so each day that you can simply work on your Ethereum investments.

LEARN AS MUCH AS POSSIBLE

People who learn more about their investments can do better with the investments that they make. This is something that is important if you want to be able to do anything with the options that you have and you will need to learn a lot about Ethereum before you invest in it. Study up and try to find out everything that there is to know about it before you try to buy into it for investing or even just for using on purchases.

DEDICATE SPACE FOR IT

The way that you are going to invest is through an application. There needs to be space on your phone or on your tablet if you want to be able to have that application. While the application is not any larger than any app that you could have – meaning that the app is not something that will take up a lot of space – you should still make sure that your phone or your tablet is prepared for the amount of data that will be coming through the application. By looking at this and making sure that you have enough space, you will know the right way to be able to trade it.

MINE IT

You can mine for Ethereum just like you can with gold or silver outside of cyberspace. You should make sure that you are aware of what you want to do and that you are getting the best experience possible. The people who mine for it are the ones who profit the most off of it. It is important to note that Ethereum is one of the easiest types of cyber currency that you can mine for. All you need is a simple operating system and the ability to make the financial choice that is done in the right way. Once you have this, you should be able to easily figure out the right way to add different options to your wallet.

SHARE IT

It is always a good idea to share that you are working with Ethereum with other people. While you may not necessarily want to share with them how much Ethereum you have, you should let them know that it something that you are doing and that you are going to be able to continue to do it. It is always a good idea to make sure that you are sharing with others to help get the word out about it and that you will be able to make the right financial choice when it comes to the money that you can make from it.

FIND RETAILERS

You can do an easy search from the application that will show you the retailers who will accept Ethereum. These are different companies, and they may have different ways that they will take the money that you have to offer them in the form of Ethereum. Make sure that you know who they are, what they can do and how much Ethereum you can pay them for the goods or services that they have for you.

ASK FOR CURRENCY

If you are struggling to find a retailer who has what you want and is going to offer you the option to pay in Ethereum, you should try to ask them if they will accept it. If they do not know what it is, this is the perfect time to share with them what Ethereum is and how they can invest in it just like you did. There are many options that are included with Ethereum so make sure that you are fully prepared to be able to get the most out of the objectives that you have.

CONSIDER TRADING IT

There is a chance that you could trade your Ethereum. In reality, that is all you're doing when you are buying goods and services with it. You can ask different people for various trade options, or you can try to make sure that you are going to get the best deal possible for your trades. You should make sure that you are going to be able to get the best experience possible. Many people may be interested in trading their goods and services for your Ethereum.

CHAPTER 9: TRADING YOUR ETHEREUM

The only thing that you can truly do with your Ethereum is traded it. Since it is not an actual form of currency, you cannot do anything major with it that would allow you to use it to spend money. This is something that will likely be different in the future but to call it anything other than trading at this point would simply be deceptive to the way that it works. Because of the way that things are set up, there is a chance that you could trade it for many different things in an online setting.

CRYPTOCURRENCY

Cryptocurrency is not currency. This is something that needs to be looked at on a deeper level because of the problems that are often associated with using it. You need to make sure that you know that the only thing that you are doing is trading with it. Yes, people trade it for money, but that just means they purchase it as if it were any other type of good that they could purchase online. The main difference is that cryptocurrency is not necessarily in "real time." It is a virtual idea, and there are no physical instances of cryptocurrency.

PAYING WITH IT

There is no doubt that you can pay with it or at least think that you are paying with it. When you decide to pay with cryptocurrency like Ethereum, you are just trading it for a different type of good or service. This is the simple aspect of it. As technologically savvy as cryptocurrency is, it is something that is detrimental because of the things that are associated with it. It goes back to times in the past when people would typically pay for something by simply trading for it. This is something that can happen very easily.

SAVING IT UP

When you are saving your Ethereum, you are simply keeping track of it so that it will be something that you can trade for money in the future. Saving Ethereum is much different than saving cash. The biggest thing that you will notice when you are saving Ethereum is that you are not going to be able to earn interest on it. In this way, it is harder to save than cash. The benefit to it, though, is that you will be able to cash in on the increased value of it over time.

TRADING IT FOR CASH

When you have finished with your Ethereum investing process, you will be able to trade that "money" in for cash. This is something that can be done relatively easily and something that you will need to make sure that you can do each time that you try to trade your money in. There are many options that will allow you to have the best experience possible and give you the chance to be able to do more with the Cryptocurrency that you currently have. It is a good idea to try to do more with it and to get the most out of it.

Looking Ahead with It

As you learn more about Ethereum and the options that are included with it, you will be able to get much more out of the experience. You need to make sure that you are always working toward doing better with Ethereum and that you are going to be able to truly adjust to the options that are included with it. As you are looking ahead toward the future of Ethereum and with the different things that are included with it, you should be able to recognize that there are many options you may be missing out on. Be sure always to try to figure out the right way to deal with Ethereum.

Tech-Only

The majority of people who choose to use Ethereum and accept it are those who are associated with technology and the IT world. This is because Ethereum is something that will only be available in the tech world. You won't ever see Ethereum for sale in a store or any other type of location. To think that you would be able to find it in those situations would lead you to believe that it is a real currency. Since it is not, it would be hard to find it outside of the Internet and in the areas, that you would find other types of currency. Despite the fact that many tech savvy people choose to use it, it is still not widely accepted at some of the most popular technology driven websites and applications. It will, though, catch on and it will be better for people who have used it in the past because it will continue to increase in the value of it.

CHOOSING WISELY

When you are choosing whether or not you are going to use Ethereum, you should make sure that you are choosing in a way that will allow you to do more with what you have. This often means that you will need to try different things and that you will be working toward building your Ethereum stash. It is always a good idea to try and make sure that you are going to get the right type of investment, but Ethereum is always a good option.

COMPARE TO BITCOIN

When you compare the Ethereum to Bitcoin, you will find that there are a lot of differences, but there are also a lot of similarities. For example, you will find that the most popular things are sometimes not always the best. Even though a lot of people use Bitcoin and it is something that tends to be extremely popular, it may not be the best option for people who want to get the most out of their collection. It is also something that can be detrimental so make sure that you are doing what you can to get what you need out of the Bitcoin and Ethereum situation.

OPTIONAL PROTECTION

Despite the fact that Ethereum is just a tool for trading, you do get some protection with it if you want. This is almost unheard of in the investing world and is something that you should take into consideration when you are looking at different options for investing your money. You need to make sure that you are prepared to invest your money and that you will be doing everything that you can to get the most out of the money that you have. It is a wise choice to add different options to your Ethereum collection and always to make sure that you are getting the most out of it.

CHAPTER 10: GROWTH WITH ETHEREUM

Since Ethereum first became available and began as something that could be measured in trade terms, it has grown. The growth is somewhat different than what has been historically happening with Bitcoin, and that is acceptable because of the various options that are offered to the people who are a part of the way that things are done with the Ethereum. As the two largest cryptocurrencies that are available on the market, it is something that has to be comparable. Taking a look at Ethereum growth, though, shows that it is steady.

INCREASING VALUE

The value of the Ethereum has been steadily increasing in the time that people have been trading it and have been using it. This is something that will change the way that people are doing things and it will also give them the chance to be able to see that they can make money. When you look at the history of the Ethereum and the prices that changed over time, you can see that it has nearly always been increasing.

If you know the right way to be able to show that Ethereum can increase in the price, you will be able to see that there are many options for Ethereum. You will also be able to see that it has a great value currently. Historically, this is the highest price that Ethereum has been at, and it will continue to rise in the coming years. The prices are great, and they can be predicted easily using the information that has been obtained from the past references. It is a good idea to decide which way Ethereum is going to go and the chances are that it will be even more valuable in the future.

SAME INTERVALS

One of the best things about the growth that has happened with Ethereum is that it has happened at steady intervals. It has not had huge spikes where it has gone up a lot in a short period and it has not had times where it did not go up at all. This has allowed it to be one of the best options for people who want to make sure that they are doing things the right way and that they are going to be able to get a lot of help from Ethereum. The intervals at which it has grown have been very equal to each other, and they have made Ethereum price reach some of the best levels that have ever been seen in a trade especially in the world of cryptocurrency.

When you look at intervals at which something increase, it is great (of course) to see that it is increasing. It is even better to see that it is increasing steadily and that it will continue to do so in the future. This is not something that has been able to happen with Bitcoin, and it has seen huge surges and points in time where it did not move at all.

No Dips

Since Ethereum has been traded, it has not dipped at all in any major ways. Throughout the day, Ethereum may change in price a few times, or it may not be able to get to the point where people had hoped it would reach but it has also been able to stay about the same on a day to day basis. It has allowed people the chance to make sure that things are going to continue to go up in the time that is going to happen in the future.

When you are looking at an investment, you don't want to see big changes. This is especially true for big dips in price and even bigger dips in value. You need to make sure that you are learning as much about the history of an investment as you can. This means that you need to look at the trading history. The trading history of Ethereum is great and is evident with all of the options that are included with it. When you are discovering the different options with Ethereum, you need to make sure that you are doing everything that you can to be able to get the best experience possible.

Returns Rising

The returns on the investment that you make with Ethereum are always going up. The rising returns mean that you will have a chance to be able to make most, if not all, of your money back when you decide to purchase Ethereum as an investment. It is important that you work to make sure that you are going to be able to get the best experience possible with Ethereum.

If you see the recorded history of the returns on investment, you will be able to see that it has gone up in the past. It will also give you the ability to make sure that you are going to get everything done that you need to be done.

The returns are one of the most important parts of Ethereum investing. Whether you are going to do it on a casual basis or you are going to do it in a way that allows you to make a very large amount of money, you will need to have some return. Without that, the point of investing will be null and will be something that can hurt your bottom line as an investor.

CHAPTER 11:
LOOKING FORWARD AT ETHEREUM

With the historic growth of Ethereum and the availability of it steadily rising, you can expect that things will be better when it comes to the growth of it. The chances are that in a very short period, Ethereum will be nearly as popular as Bitcoin. This isn't to say that everyone is going to have a piece of the Ethereum pie, but it does say a lot for the things that are going to happen and for the various options that are going to work with the people who are buying different things on the Internet. When you are considering investing in something as simple as the cryptocurrency, you need to make sure that you are prepared for how complicated it can get.

OVERCOMING BITCOIN

The first step that Ethereum will need to make is overcoming Bitcoin. Bitcoin is the popular option of cryptocurrency, and it is also the fastest growing option that is available. There are several other small cryptocurrencies available, but these have not seen growth in the way that Bitcoin has. In fact, they haven't even seen the same level of growth that has been seen with Ethereum.

Increased Popularity

As the popularity of Ethereum increases, the more it will become even more popular. In many instances, this means that people will need to make the choice that they have with other options included in their investment portfolio. In other instances, it means that people will need to do more with the life that they are living and with the investments that they have put into place. It is a good idea to see how the popularity will change the way that things are done and how it will make most things better for people who have already invested in Ethereum.

Options in Retail

It is not unheard of to see something blow up quickly like Bitcoin did. While the chances are small for the same thing to happen with Ethereum, it can happen. The real indicator of whether something has "made it" regarding popularity is when it is seen in retail locations. There are very limited instances of Bitcoin in retail locations, but there are more that are being added on a regular basis. This is expected to happen with Ethereum, too.

Some Brick and Mortar

Despite the fact that Ethereum and other cryptocurrencies are mainly used in the cyber world, there are options that are included with brick and mortar locations. It is important to note that it may be harder to pay with something like Ethereum or even with Bitcoin. Better technology that is offered in real stores is something that is going to make this more of a possibility in the future. It is also something that will make things better for the people who have already invested in Ethereum.

DIFFERENT OPTIONS IN TRADING

As Ethereum continues to grow in popularity and more people become interested in it, the trading options will increase and will start to see a major shift in the way that they are done. If you did trading with Ethereum in the past, the chances are that within a few years' time; it will be completely different from what it currently is. There are so many different ways that people can make the change from the original trades that they did to the new way of trading. It is going to change again shortly when Ethereum hits peak popularity.

THE VALUE GOES UP

When all of this starts to take place, and once it begins to become more popular, the value of Ethereum will increase. This happens with nearly everything that is investible and is something that will make new options for people who have not had the chance to invest in the past. It is important for new investors to look at the various options and for them to recognize that they are going to be able to benefit from all of the things that are associated with investing and with

Ethereum in general. It is always a good idea to try and do more with what you have, and Ethereum allows people the chance to do it.

CONCLUSION

Thank for making it through to the end of Ethereum Investing. Let's hope it was informative and able to provide you with all of the tools you need to achieve your goals of making money from something that is online and being able to grow passive income as a result of the investments that you have made in Ethereum.

The next step is to download the Ethereum app and try to find out as much about it as you can before you invest in it.

Finally, if you found this book useful in any way, a review on Amazon is always appreciated!

www.ingramcontent.com/pod-product-compliance
Lightning Source LLC
Chambersburg PA
CBHW051246170526
45165CB00004B/1590